# CALABRIA TOUR GUIDE 2025:

## Exploring Italy's Southern Jewel, From Ancient Ruins to Modern Charms

David S. Wexler

# Table Of Contents

# How to Scan the QR Codes in This Book

1. **Open QR Scanner:** Launch a QR code scanning app on your smartphone. If your phone's camera app can scan QR codes, open the camera.

**2. Position the QR Code:** Hold your phone steady and position the QR code within the frame on your screen. Make sure the entire QR code is visible.

**3. Focus:** Ensure your camera is focused on the QR code. Some apps automatically concentrate, while others may need manual adjustment.

**4. Wait for Recognition:** Keep your phone steady and wait for the app to recognize the QR code. This usually takes just a moment.

**5. Read the Content:** Once the QR code is recognized, your phone will take you to the exact location on Google Maps. Enter your current location to get accurate directions to that destination.

# Introduction

## Welcome to Calabria

Calabria has always been a wonderful place for me. Located at the tip of Italy's "boot," it wasn't as famous as Tuscany or the Amalfi Coast. But the hidden villages, rugged coastlines, and old traditions intrigued me, and I decided to explore this lesser-known gem. As soon as I arrived, I knew I made the right choice.

My adventure started in Reggio Calabria, the southernmost part facing the Strait of Messina. On my first morning, I walked along Lungomare Falcomatà, known as "the most beautiful kilometer in Italy." With palm trees swaying, the breeze from the sea, and Sicily in the distance, it felt like a postcard came to life. The place had an untouched charm, with locals enjoying espresso at outdoor cafés.

The highlight came when I visited the National Archaeological Museum of Reggio Calabria to see the Riace Bronzes. These 5th-century BC statues were so detailed that they seemed almost alive. Standing before them, I could feel the deep history of Calabria, a land shaped by the Greeks, Romans, Byzantines, and Normans.

Next, I traveled inland to Gerace, a medieval village that seemed frozen in time. As I walked its cobbled streets toward the ancient Norman Castle, the view of olive groves and the Ionian Sea was breathtaking. In Gerace Cathedral, one of southern Italy's largest, I felt the weight of centuries of history.

In Stilo, I discovered the Cattolica Church, a stunning example of Byzantine architecture, with red domes and preserved frescoes. The town, nestled at the base of Monte Consolino, was full of life, especially during a festival for the town's patron saint. I even joined the locals in dancing the Tarantella, a joyful folk dance.

Another highlight was the cliffside town of Tropea, known as the "Pearl of the Tyrrhenian." The views were breathtaking, with buildings perched on cliffs above the sea. I relaxed on Spiaggia di Tropea, a beach with crystal-clear water, and climbed to the Sanctuary of Santa Maria dell'Isola, where I enjoyed stunning views of the coastline.

Calabria's food was unforgettable. I tried 'nduja, a spicy spreadable salami, and dined on swordfish in Cosenza, paired with the local wine, Cirò. Every meal was a discovery, from traditional stews to fresh pasta and even the simple but delicious gelato.

Calabria is also perfect for nature lovers. I hiked in Aspromonte National Park, with its rugged mountains and untouched forests. The scenery was wild and beautiful, with waterfalls and wildflowers along the way.

By the end of my journey, I realized that Calabria was more than just a place—it was an experience. Its people, food, and history left a lasting impression on me.

## Brief History of Calabria

Calabria, located at the "toe" of Italy's boot, was once called Bruttium, named after the native Bruttii people who lived there long before the Romans arrived. These early inhabitants were independent and skilled in warfare, forming a unique identity before the Greeks came.

In the 8th century BCE, the Greeks founded colonies in Calabria, turning cities like Rhegion (now Reggio Calabria) and Locri into important centers of Greek culture, art, and philosophy. Walking through these ancient cities, you would have seen temples, theaters, and bustling marketplaces. The Greek influence still lives on today in Calabria's language and food.

As Greek power declined, the Romans moved in. By 272 BCE, after several wars, Calabria became part of the Roman Empire. Under Roman rule, roads like the Via Popilia connected the region to Rome, boosting trade. However, Calabria often stayed on the edge of Roman society, keeping parts of its native traditions.

When the Roman Empire fell in the 5th century CE, Calabria went through a rough period. Invaders like the Visigoths, Byzantines, and Lombards fought for control, and the region became isolated. During Byzantine rule, starting in the 6th century, Calabria regained some importance with the rise of monasteries and Christian influence, leaving behind a legacy still visible in its old churches.

In the 9th and 10th centuries, Arab and Saracen raids caused chaos, and many coastal areas were fortified. It wasn't until the Normans arrived in the 11th century that Calabria found some stability, becoming part of the Kingdom of Sicily and later the Kingdom of Naples.

Through the Middle Ages, Calabria suffered from poverty and natural disasters like the earthquake in 1783. The region remained on the outskirts of Italian politics but held on to a strong sense of identity. In the 19th century, during Italy's unification, Calabria joined the fight for independence, but it remained poor, leading many people to emigrate.

Today, Calabria still faces challenges like economic difficulties and the influence of the 'Ndrangheta crime syndicate. Despite this, the region remains proud of its history and culture, showing a strong connection to its past while moving forward into the future.

# 10 Reasons to Visit Calabria as your Next Vacation Destination

### 1. Beautiful, Untouched Beaches

Imagine relaxing on soft, golden sand with the sun warming your skin and the clear blue Mediterranean stretching out in front of you. Calabria's beaches are some of the most beautiful in Italy and remain largely untouched by large crowds. Whether you're drawn to the dramatic cliffs of Tropea or the peaceful shores of Capo Vaticano, Calabria offers perfect spots for swimming, sunbathing, and enjoying the clear waters of the Tyrrhenian and Ionian Seas.

### 2. Delicious Italian Food

Calabria is a haven for food enthusiasts. Here, you can savor authentic southern Italian dishes, from spicy 'nduja sausage to fresh seafood and homemade pasta. The local cuisine is known for its bold flavors and use of fresh, local ingredients like olive oil, chili peppers, and citrus fruits. Don't miss traditional dishes like pasta alla 'nduja, swordfish, or 'nduja-stuffed peppers. You'll also find excellent gelato in Tropea and local wines from Calabria's vineyards. Each meal celebrates the region's agricultural traditions.

### 3. Rich History and Culture

Calabria's long history is reflected in its architecture, ancient ruins, and enduring local traditions. Once part of Magna Graecia, you can explore Greek temples, Roman ruins, and medieval castles in cities like Reggio Calabria, Cosenza, and Stilo. Visit the Riace Bronzes, ancient Greek statues in Reggio Calabria's National Archaeological Museum, or stroll through the medieval village of Gerace for a taste of the past.

### 4. Stunning Natural Landscapes

Calabria is a paradise for nature lovers, offering everything from mountains and forests to beautiful coastlines. Sila National Park features dense forests, lakes, and high-altitude plains ideal for hiking, cycling, and winter sports. Aspromonte National Park offers rugged mountains, waterfalls, and wildlife with trails leading to breathtaking sea views. If you love outdoor adventures, Calabria's parks are perfect for exploring its wild beauty.

## 5. Charming Small Towns

Calabria is home to picturesque villages where life feels like it hasn't changed in centuries. Towns like Scilla, perched on a cliff overlooking the sea, and Stilo with its famous Cattolica church, offer charming streets and stunning views. These small towns let you experience the slower pace of Calabrian life, where you can find artisan shops, historic churches, and traditional crafts like ceramics and lace-making.

## 6. Spectacular Coastlines

Calabria boasts both Ionian and Tyrrhenian coastlines, each with its unique appeal. The Tyrrhenian beaches, such as Tropea and Pizzo, are known for their dramatic cliffs and clear waters, while the Ionian coast features long sandy shores. Spend your days relaxing on the beach, swimming in the crystal-clear sea, or sailing to explore hidden coves and marine reserves. Calabria's beaches are less crowded than those in other parts of Italy, offering a peaceful retreat.

## 7. *Affordable Luxury*

Calabria offers great value compared to more famous destinations like Rome or Venice. Whether you're enjoying a multi-course meal at a local trattoria or staying in a luxurious seaside resort, you'll find that your money goes further here. Calabria's authenticity means you can enjoy an unspoiled version of Italy without paying the high prices often associated with more tourist-heavy regions.

## 8. *Friendly Locals*

Calabrians are known for their warmth and hospitality. Even if you don't speak much Italian, you'll find locals eager to make you feel welcome, often inviting you to share a meal or stories. Whether chatting with a shop owner, winemaker, or local fisherman, you'll leave feeling like you've made new friends. The friendly nature of the people adds to the charm of your stay.

### 9. Year-Round Appeal

Thanks to its Mediterranean climate, Calabria is a great destination all year long. Summer is perfect for beach days and water activities, while spring and fall are ideal for exploring the region's villages, parks, and historic sites without the heat. Even winter has its charm, with Christmas markets and local holiday festivals. Calabria's diverse landscapes and activities ensure there's something to enjoy in every season.

### 10. A Hidden Gem

If you want to avoid the crowds and explore a less-known destination, Calabria is perfect. While popular spots like Amalfi or Tuscany attract millions of tourists, Calabria remains refreshingly off the beaten path. Here, you can experience Italy's beauty without the usual tourist hustle, making for a more peaceful and authentic travel experience. Calabria lets you immerse yourself in Italy's culture, history, and nature on your terms.

# Chapter 1

# Planning Your Trip to Calabria

## Best Time to Visit

Calabria is beautiful year-round, but the time you choose to visit can shape your experience. If you're after sunny beaches, cultural festivals, or outdoor adventures, understanding the seasons will help you plan your trip.

**Spring (March to May) – Perfect for Nature Lovers and Culture Seekers**

Spring is a wonderful time to visit if you prefer fewer tourists. As the weather warms, wildflowers bloom, and temperatures range from 15°C to 20°C (59°F to 68°F). It's great for hiking in places like Sila National Park or the Aspromonte mountains. You'll also find Easter processions and other cultural festivals that highlight the region's rich traditions. Coastal towns like Tropea and Scilla are peaceful, though the water may still be too cold for swimming.

## Summer (June to August) – Best for Beach Lovers

If you love the beach, summer is the best time to visit Calabria. The coastline along the Ionian and Tyrrhenian seas offers warm temperatures of 25°C to 35°C (77°F to 95°F), perfect for swimming and sunbathing. Popular beaches like Tropea and Capo Vaticano are ideal for relaxation and water activities, though they can get crowded. Local festivals and food events also take place, adding to the lively atmosphere.

## Fall (September to November) – Ideal for Foodies and Outdoor Enthusiasts

Autumn in Calabria is a peaceful time, with warm temperatures lasting through September. You can still enjoy the beaches and explore the countryside with cooler temperatures of 10°C to 18°C (50°F to 64°F). It's also the harvest season, with opportunities for wine tastings and food festivals, like the Chestnut Festival in Mammola.

### Winter (December to February) – A Quiet, Cultural Escape

Winter offers a quieter experience, with mild temperatures around 10°C to 15°C (50°F to 59°F) along the coast. While beach days are over, it's the perfect time to explore historic towns like Gerace or enjoy winter sports in Sila National Park. If you visit during Christmas, you'll experience local festive traditions and markets.

## What to Pack for Your Trip to Calabria

Here's a simple guide to help you pack smart:

## 1. Clothes for Warm Weather

Calabria has a Mediterranean climate, especially along the coast, where summer temperatures can reach the mid-80s or higher. Pack lightweight, breathable clothes like cotton or linen. Bring short-sleeve tops, tank tops, and light long-sleeve shirts for sun protection or cool evenings. Comfortable shorts and light pants will keep you cool while exploring towns and the countryside.

In late spring or early autumn, the weather is milder, but still warm. Pack summer clothes with light layers, like a cardigan or scarf, as evenings can be cooler by the coast. A light jacket or sweater is also useful for breezy nights.

## 2. Swimwear and Beach Items

Calabria's coastline is stunning, with spots like Tropea and Capo Vaticano. Pack at least two swimsuits, a beach cover-up, and a wide-brimmed hat or cap for sun protection. Sunglasses are a must. Bring a light beach towel or sarong, as not all beaches have loungers for rent. Flip-flops or sandals are great for the beach.

### 3. Comfortable Walking Shoes

Calabria's towns, like Gerace and Reggio Calabria, are best explored on foot. Bring comfortable shoes or sandals for walking on cobbled streets and uneven surfaces. Sneakers are perfect for longer walks or exploring historic sites with steep streets. For hiking in places like Aspromonte or Sila National Parks, pack sturdy hiking shoes.

### 4. Activewear for Outdoor Adventures

Calabria offers great hiking and outdoor activities. Pack breathable, moisture-wicking clothes like quick-dry pants or shorts and a light jacket, especially if you're heading to the mountains where the weather can change quickly. Don't forget a reusable water bottle to stay hydrated.

### 5. Sun Protection

The sun in Calabria can be strong, especially in the summer. Pack high-SPF sunscreen, and SPF lip balm, and consider a small sun umbrella if you're sensitive to the sun.

## 6. Useful Accessories

A small crossbody bag or backpack is great for carrying essentials like sunscreen, water, and your phone. A scarf or shawl is useful for visiting religious sites and covering your shoulders, and it can double as a stylish accessory.

## 7. Power Adapters and Electronics

Italy uses Type C, F, and L plugs, so bring a travel adapter to charge your devices. A portable charger is also handy for long days out. Don't forget your smartphone for photos and navigation or a camera for capturing beautiful landscapes.

## 8. Medications and First Aid

Bring any prescription medications, plus a basic first-aid kit with bandages, antiseptic, and over-the-counter meds like painkillers or motion sickness pills. If you're heading into nature, insect repellent is a good idea.

### 9. Important Travel Documents

MPackyour passport, travel insurance, and any reservation details. A travel wallet or organizer can help keep everything together and easily accessible.

# How to Reach Calabria

Planning a trip to Calabria is easy, with several ways to reach this beautiful region in southern Italy. You can travel by plane, train, car, or even ferry, depending on your preferences and budget.

### By Plane

Flying is the fastest way to get to Calabria, and there are three main airports to choose from:

- Lamezia Terme International Airport (SUF) is the largest and most convenient, offering both domestic flights from cities like Rome and Milan and international flights from places like London and Munich. Budget airlines such as Ryanair and easyJet fly here often.

- Reggio Calabria Airport (REG), located in the south, is a good choice if you're visiting coastal areas like Reggio Calabria or Scilla. It mainly offers domestic flights.
- Crotone Airport (CRV) is smaller but ideal for visiting the Ionian coast or nearby towns. It mostly has flights from cities like Rome and Milan.

After landing, renting a car is recommended for exploring the area, but you can also find buses and taxis to take you to nearby towns.

**By Train**

If you're traveling from within Italy or nearby countries, taking the train is a scenic and stress-free way to get to Calabria. Trenitalia operates high-speed trains like the Frecciarossa and Frecciargento, which can take you from Rome to Reggio Calabria in about five hours.

For a more relaxed, scenic journey, InterCity trains are a slower option but offer views of Italy's diverse landscapes as you travel south.

**By Car**

Driving to Calabria offers the freedom to explore at your own pace. If you're coming from northern or central Italy, take the Autostrada A1 from cities like Florence or Rome, and then connect to the Autostrada A2 to reach Calabria. This route provides stunning views of the Mediterranean and Calabrian mountains.

Having a car also makes it easier to visit remote areas, such as Sila National Park, or small towns like Gerace. Just be prepared for narrow, winding roads, especially in the mountains.

**By Ferry**

If you're coming from Sicily or other Mediterranean locations, a ferry is a scenic way to arrive. Ferries run regularly between Messina in Sicily and Villa San Giovanni or Reggio Calabria, with crossings taking about 30 minutes. You can also bring your car on board to continue your road trip.

## Getting Around Calabria

There are several ways to get around Calabria,

let's dive into it:


**Public Transport: Trains and Buses**

Calabria's public transportation is affordable
and covers many areas, although it might not be
the fastest option. The main cities like Reggio
Calabria, Cosenza, Catanzaro, and Lamezia
Terme are connected by Trenitalia trains. These
trains are comfortable, and the coastal routes
offer stunning views of the Ionian and
Tyrrhenian seas. However, expect occasional
delays.

For smaller towns or rural areas, buses are the
best option. Companies like Autolinee Federico
and SAJ provide bus services across the region.
Buses are reliable and cheap, but they run less
frequently on weekends and holidays. It's a
good idea to check the schedules in advance.


**Renting a Car: Freedom to Explore**

Renting a car is the best way to explore
Calabria at your own pace, especially if you
want to visit remote areas or hidden spots.
Major rental companies like Hertz, Avis, and

Europcar are available in the main cities and at Lamezia Terme Airport.

Most roads in Calabria are in good condition, but driving in narrow hilltop towns or along winding coastal roads can be tricky. The main highway, the A2, connects cities like Reggio Calabria and Cosenza. While rural roads can be slow and narrow, they offer a chance to see the authentic side of Calabria. Just be cautious, as local drivers can be fast and aggressive.

**Taxis and Ridesharing**

Taxis are available in cities but can be expensive for long trips. You'll usually find taxis at stands or train stations, or you can call for one. Make sure the meter is running or agree on a price before starting the trip. Ridesharing services like Uber aren't common in Calabria, so you'll likely need to rely on taxis or private car services, especially in more remote areas.

**Cycling and Walking: For the Adventurous**

If you enjoy cycling, Calabria's rugged terrain offers great routes along the coast and in parks like Aspromonte and Sila. You can rent bikes locally, and some companies offer guided tours. Walking is a great way to explore small towns like Tropea, Gerace, and Scilla. You can also enjoy hiking trails, which range from easy walks to tougher mountain treks. If you plan on hiking, be sure to bring sturdy shoes.

**Ferries and Boats: Exploring the Coast**

You can also explore Calabria's coastline by ferry or boat. Ferries connect Calabria with Sicily and the Aeolian Islands, with services from Reggio Calabria and Villa San Giovanni. Boat tours are available along the Tyrrhenian coast, offering stunning views of cliffs, caves, and clear waters.

# Visa and Entry Requirements

Calabria follows Italy's national visa rules as part of the European Union (EU) and the Schengen Area. What you need depends on your nationality, how long you plan to stay, and the purpose of your visit. Here's a simple breakdown of what to know:

## Who Needs a Visa?

- *EU, EEA, and Swiss citizens:* No visa is needed to enter Calabria or Italy, and you can stay as long as you like with a valid ID or passport. UK citizens can also visit without a visa, but if staying for more than 90 days, further requirements apply.

- *Non-EU citizens (like those from the US, Canada, Australia, and Japan):* You can visit Calabria and the Schengen Area without a visa for up to 90 days within 180 days. But if you plan to stay longer or for purposes like work or study, you'll need a visa from an Italian consulate before traveling.

## ETIAS Authorization

From 2025, citizens of visa-exempt countries will need an ETIAS (European Travel Information and Authorization System) before entering Italy or any Schengen country. It's not a visa, but an online authorization that's easy to apply for and is valid for up to three years.

## Documents Required for Entry

Regardless of whether you need a visa, you'll

need these documents:

1. Valid passport (must be valid for at least three months beyond your stay).

2. Proof of onward travel (such as a return flight).

3. Proof of accommodation (hotel booking or invitation from a host).

4. Sufficient funds (bank statements or credit cards to show you can support yourself).

5. Travel insurance (recommended to cover medical expenses).

## Extending Your Stay or Long-Term Visas

If you want to stay longer than 90 days, you'll need to apply for a long-term visa before traveling. After arriving, apply for a residence permit within eight days.

## Penalties for Overstaying

Be sure to follow the visa rules. Overstaying can lead to fines, deportation, or bans from re-entering the Schengen Area.

# Currency and Money Matters

Italy, including Calabria, uses the euro (€) as its only currency. Here's a simple guide to handling money during your stay.

## Currency Basics

The euro is divided into 100 cents. You'll use coins from 1 cent to €2 and banknotes from €5 to €500. While small businesses and rural places may prefer cash, credit and debit cards are widely accepted in cities like Reggio Calabria, Catanzaro, and Cosenza, especially in restaurants, hotels, and stores. It's a good idea to have some cash on hand for small purchases and tips, but you don't need large amounts for daily expenses.

## Exchanging Money

If you bring foreign currency, you'll need to exchange it for euros. You can do this at airports, train stations, or banks, but ATMs and online banking apps often have better exchange rates and lower fees. If you use a currency exchange booth, watch out for high commission fees.

Let your bank or credit card company know about your travel plans to avoid any issues with transactions being blocked.

## Using ATMs

ATMs (called "bancomats" in Italy) are common in Calabria, especially in cities and tourist areas. They usually offer the best exchange rates for withdrawing euros with your debit or credit card. Most ATMs accept major cards like Visa, MasterCard, and American Express. You'll find them near banks, airports, and train stations.

Be aware that your home bank may charge fees for international withdrawals, and local banks might add their fees. Check with your bank before traveling to avoid surprises. Use ATMs from well-known banks like Intesa Sanpaolo, UniCredit, or Banco di Napoli for safer transactions and possibly lower fees.

## Tipping and Payment Etiquette

Tipping isn't expected in Calabria but is

appreciated. In restaurants, a small service charge, called "coperto," is often added to your bill. If you're happy with the service, a 5-10% tip in cash is customary. For taxis, round up to the nearest euro, and for hotel staff, a few euros for good service is polite.

Credit cards are accepted in most places but always ask before assuming. Some small towns may not accept cards, so carry some cash just in case. Contactless payments are becoming more common, but cash is still preferred in many areas.

**VAT and Tax Refunds**

If you're not an EU resident, you might be able to get a VAT refund on certain purchases. The standard VAT rate in Italy is 22%. To qualify, you need to spend at least €154.94 in one store on the same day and request a VAT refund form. Keep your passport with you when making large purchases. When you leave the EU, show your VAT refund form, purchases, and receipts at customs to get your refund.

# Chapter 2

# Exploring Calabria's Major Cities

## Reggio Calabria

Reggio Calabria, the largest city in Calabria, sits at the southern tip of Italy, right along the Tyrrhenian Sea. Known for its stunning views of the Strait of Messina, you can see the outline of Sicily across the water.

One of the city's main attractions is the Archaeological Museum, which houses the famous Riace Bronzes—two ancient Greek warrior statues discovered off the coast. These are considered masterpieces of Greek art and are a must-see. The museum also offers many artifacts from ancient times, giving visitors a glimpse into Calabria's past.

The Lungomare Falcomatà, known as "Italy's most beautiful kilometer," is a scenic walkway along the coast, lined with palm trees, restaurants, and cafes. The views of the sea and the Sicilian mountains are especially breathtaking at sunset, making it a popular place for both locals and tourists to relax and enjoy the atmosphere.

Another important site is Reggio Calabria Cathedral, the largest church in the region. Its architecture blends styles from different periods, and the inside is decorated with beautiful frescoes and sculptures, offering a peaceful escape from the busy city.

For art lovers, Villa Zerbi hosts various exhibitions, and the National Gallery displays works by local artists.

Food in Reggio Calabria is also worth trying. Local dishes include 'nduja, a spicy sausage spread, and swordfish, a common ingredient in Calabrian cuisine. The city's many restaurants serve fresh seafood and traditional dishes, providing a delicious taste of the region.

# Cosenza

Cosenza, often known as the "Athens of Calabria" for its rich history and vibrant culture, Cosenza blends its ancient past with a lively modern art scene, making it a must-see for travelers.

At the heart of Cosenza is its old town, with narrow, winding streets that showcase centuries of architecture and culture. The centerpiece is the Cosenza Cathedral, a UNESCO World Heritage site from the 11th century, with a Romanesque exterior and Gothic interior. Nearby, Piazza XV Marzo features a statue of local philosopher Bernardino Telesio and is home to cultural landmarks like Teatro Rendano, the largest opera house in Calabria.

Cosenza's history is also on display at the Norman-Swabian Castle, sitting on a hill overlooking the city. Built by the Byzantines in the 10th century and expanded by Frederick II in the 13th, the castle offers stunning views of the city and countryside, making it perfect for photography or a quiet moment.

For art lovers, the Bilotti Open-Air Museum on Corso Mazzini is a unique attraction, featuring sculptures by famous artists like Salvador Dalí and Giorgio de Chirico. As you walk along this lively street, you can shop at local stores and enjoy the vibrant café scene.

Food is another highlight of Cosenza, with local dishes like "lagane e cicciari" (pasta with chickpeas) and "soppressata" (cured meat) taking center stage. The city is also known for its bold red wines, especially from the Savuto and Donnici regions.

## Catanzaro

Catanzaro is often called the "City of Two Seas" because it's close to both the Ionian and Tyrrhenian coasts, making it a great starting point to explore Calabria's landscapes. Positioned between the Sila mountains and the coast, Catanzaro offers visitors a mix of historical sites, beautiful views, and local traditions.

Founded by the Byzantines in the 9th century, Catanzaro has a rich history that includes Norman, Swabian, and Spanish influences. You can see this past in the city's architecture, like the Scolacium Archaeological Park just outside the city, which has ancient Roman ruins, including an amphitheater and basilica. The Norman Castle, built in the 11th century, is another important site. Even though it's partly in ruins, it offers great views and a glimpse into the city's medieval past.

Catanzaro is also known for its green spaces. Villa Trieste is a beautiful garden in the city where you can take a relaxing walk and enjoy views of the area. If you're looking for some time by the sea, Catanzaro Lido offers lovely beaches and seaside restaurants with fresh seafood.

The city has a long tradition of silk-making, once making it a major silk hub in Italy. While this has decreased over the years, you can still find artisans crafting fine fabrics today.

For art lovers, the Museo delle Arti di Catanzaro (MARCA) is a must-see, featuring both modern and traditional art from Calabria.

Catanzaro also hosts various festivals throughout the year, including religious events, food festivals, and the popular Magna Graecia Film Festival, which celebrates Italian cinema.

## Lamezia Terme

The city mixes old and new, with ancient Greek, Roman, and Norman influences seen in its architecture and ruins. One highlight is the Norman-Swabian Castle, which sits on a hill with great views of the area. Though partly in ruins, it shows the city's importance during the Middle Ages. Close by is the Bastion of the Knights of Malta, another historical landmark.

For those interested in religious history, Lamezia Terme has the Sanctuary of St. Antonio di Padova, a popular church for pilgrims, and the Church of San Domenico, known for its beautiful Baroque architecture and frescoes.

Lamezia Terme is also famous for its natural hot springs. The Terme di Caronte, located just outside the city, offers relaxing baths in mineral-rich waters that have been used for healing for centuries, all set against a backdrop of mountains and greenery.

The city is a great base for exploring Calabria's coastline. The nearby Tyrrhenian beaches, like Gizzeria Lido, are known for their golden sands and clear waters. Gizzeria is also a hotspot for windsurfing and kitesurfing.

Lamezia Terme is part of Calabria's growing wine scene, producing unique wines like Greco and Gaglioppo. Visitors can tour the local vineyards and enjoy tastings.

# Chapter 3

# Hidden Gems of Calabria

## Scilla: Mythical Landscapes and the Legend of Charybdis

Scilla is famous for its role in the Greek myth of Scylla and Charybdis from Homer's Odyssey. In the legend, Scylla was a monster with twelve heads and six rows of teeth, while Charybdis was a giant whirlpool that swallows ships. They were said to live on opposite sides of a narrow strait, making it dangerous for sailors. This strait is thought to be the Strait of Messina, which separates Italy from Sicily. The dramatic cliffs and clear blue waters of Scilla bring these ancient stories to life, making it a great spot for mythology enthusiasts.

The village itself features a blend of rugged coastline and traditional buildings. The most notable landmark is Ruffo Castle, which sits on a cliff overlooking the sea. This medieval fortress offers amazing views and is a fantastic place for photos. Scilla also boasts beautiful beaches like Spiaggia di Scilla, where you can swim and sunbathe in clear waters surrounded by rocky outcrops and small coves.

**Getting to Scilla is easy, with several travel options:**

- *By Train:* You can take a train on the Reggio Calabria-Siderno line, with regular services from cities like Reggio Calabria and Messina. It's a short walk or taxi ride from the station to the town and beach.
- *By Car:* Driving gives you the freedom to explore at your own pace. Scilla is about 25 kilometers southwest of Reggio Calabria, and the drive offers scenic views. There's plenty of parking available.
- *By Bus:* Regional buses connect Scilla with other parts of Calabria and Sicily, arriving in the town center where you can easily reach the main attractions.
- *By Ferry:* In the summer, ferries run between Scilla and Sicilian ports like Messina, providing a scenic and breezy approach to the village.

## Tropea: The Jewel of the Tyrrhenian Sea

Tropea is often called the "Gem of the Tyrrhenian Sea." With its stunning views of clear blue waters, beautiful beaches, and charming old streets, Tropea offers a perfect Mediterranean experience.

The town's historic center features narrow, cobblestone streets lined with old buildings and lively shops. A key landmark is the Sanctuary of Santa Maria dell'Isola, an 11th-century monastery on a rocky promontory with breathtaking sea views.

Tropea is famous for its beaches, especially Spiaggia di Tropea, known for its soft white sand and clear, shallow waters perfect for swimming. The nearby beaches of Capo Vaticano and Grotticelle offer quieter spots with clear waters and fewer crowds.

The town is also a culinary delight, famous for its sweet red onions used in local dishes. Fresh seafood, homemade pasta, and local wines are also highlights of Calabrian cuisine.

Tropea's rich history is reflected in its architecture, with influences from the Normans and Swabians. Annual events like the Tropea Music Festival and Onion Festival showcase local traditions and celebrations.

**Getting to Tropea:**
Traveling to Tropea is relatively easy with several options:

- *By Air:* The nearest major airport is Lamezia Terme International Airport (SUF), about 60 kilometers (37 miles)

away. From there, you can rent a car or take a train or bus to Tropea, which takes roughly an hour by car, with other options taking a bit longer.

- *By Train:* Tropea is accessible by train from major cities like Rome and Naples. The train station is close to the town center, making it easy to get to your accommodation.
- *By Car:* Driving allows you to explore Calabria's beautiful landscape. Tropea is reachable via the A3 Autostrada del Mediterraneo, with parking available around the town.
- *By Bus:* Buses from major Italian cities to Tropea are available. This option is often more budget-friendly but may be less flexible compared to driving or taking the train.

## Gerace: Medieval Charm in the Aspromonte Mountains

Gerace's main attraction is its impressive Norman castle, which highlights the town's historical importance. The castle's strong walls and tall towers provide stunning views of the Aspromonte Mountains and the Ionian Sea. Walking around the castle lets visitors experience a piece of history, imagining life in the medieval era.

Next to the castle is the Gerace Cathedral, or Cattedrale di Gerace. This 11th-century Romanesque cathedral features beautiful architecture and a striking Byzantine fresco in

its apse. Its bell tower, visible from many parts of town, is a key feature of Gerace's skyline and represents the town's historical and spiritual importance.

Gerace is also known for its charming narrow streets lined with stone houses, traditional shops, and cozy cafes. Exploring these streets reveals hidden corners and lovely squares that feel timeless, offering a pleasant escape from the modern world.

The town hosts various festivals throughout the year, including the "Sagra del Vino e del Peperoncino," a lively event celebrating local wine and chili peppers. This festival is a great way to experience Calabrian food, music, and culture.

**Getting to Gerace**

- *By Car:* Driving to Gerace is the easiest option. From Reggio Calabria, it's about an hour and a half via the A2 motorway.

Take the A2 north, exit for Gerace, and follow the signs. The drive through the Aspromonte Mountains is scenic.

- *By Train:* You can also take a train from Reggio Calabria to Locri, which is 20 kilometers from Gerace. From Locri, take a taxi or local bus to Gerace. The train ride offers a comfortable and scenic route.
- *By Bus:* Regional buses connect Reggio Calabria and other major towns with Gerace. Although bus service is less frequent, it's another option to consider. Check schedules in advance as they can vary.

## Stilo: Byzantine Architecture and the Cattolica Church

Stilo is famous for its stunning landscapes and historic buildings, especially the Cattolica Church. This 9th-century church is a beautiful example of Byzantine architecture and one of the best-preserved in Southern Italy.

The Cattolica Church, or Chiesa della Cattolica, has a simple yet striking design. It has a rectangular shape with a central dome supported by four large arches. Inside, you'll find beautiful frescoes and intricate carvings that showcase Byzantine art. The vivid colors and detailed images reflect the church's spiritual significance and Orthodox Christian heritage. The peaceful atmosphere makes it a perfect place for reflection and appreciation.

Stilo is a charming town nestled in the Aspromonte Mountains, offering breathtaking views and a serene setting. As you wander through its narrow streets, you'll see medieval buildings, ancient ruins, and cozy local cafes where you can taste Calabrian specialties. Beyond the Cattolica Church, you can explore nearby sites like the Norman Castle ruins and the Convent of San Francesco.

**Getting to Stilo**

Travelers can reach Stilo through various transportation options. The nearest major cities are Reggio Calabria and Catanzaro.

- *By Car:* Renting a car is a convenient way to explore Calabria at your own pace. From Reggio Calabria, take the A2 motorway toward Lamezia Terme. After about 70 kilometers, exit for Stilo and follow the signs. The drive offers scenic views of Calabria's countryside and coast.
- *By Train:* For those who prefer public transport, regular trains run from Reggio

Calabria to Stilo. You can also take a train to Bovalino or Roccella Jonica, then catch a taxi or local bus to Stilo. This provides a relaxing journey through the beautiful Calabrian landscape.

- *By Bus:* Direct buses from Catanzaro and Reggio Calabria also serve Stilo. Check bus schedules in advance to plan your trip.

## Sila National Park

Located in the heart of Calabria, Sila National Park is a stunning destination for nature lovers and adventure seekers. Covering about 74,000 hectares, this park features a variety of landscapes, including lush forests, rolling hills, peaceful lakes, and rugged mountains. It's perfect for anyone looking to enjoy both relaxation and adventure in the beautiful nature of southern Italy.

Sila National Park is known for its diverse wildlife. Its forests, filled with beech, fir, and pine trees, provide a habitat for animals like deer, wild boar, and the rare European wolf.

Bird watchers will also enjoy spotting golden eagles and peregrine falcons.

A highlight of the park is the Sila Plateau, a high area offering breathtaking views of the surroundings. Here, you'll find Sila Grande, the park's highest peak at over 1,900 meters. The plateau has various hiking trails, from easy walks to challenging climbs, each providing unique views of the park's beauty.

**Getting There**

Getting to Sila National Park is fairly easy, though planning ahead helps.

- *By Car:* The park is accessible by car from major Calabrian cities. From Cosenza, take the SS107 highway east toward the park. From Catanzaro, follow SS280 to SS107. Look for signs leading to various park entrances.
- *By Train and Bus:* The nearest major train stations are in Cosenza or Lamezia Terme. From these cities, take a regional bus to the park's visitor centers or nearby towns like Camigliatello Silano or Lorica. Buses might not run frequently, so check schedules in advance.
- *By Air:* The closest airports are Lamezia Terme International Airport (SUF) and Reggio Calabria Airport (REG). Renting a car from the airport is the easiest way to reach the park. Alternatively, you can use public transport to travel to Cosenza or Lamezia Terme and then take a bus.

# Chapter 4

# Dining and Nightlife

## Top 10 Must-Try Local Food in Calabria

Here are the top 10 foods every traveler should try:

### 1. 'Nduja

A famous Calabrian spreadable pork sausage, 'nduja is known for its spicy kick. Made with pork, fat, and lots of chili peppers, it's perfect on bread, pasta, or pizza.

### 2. Sardella

Sardella, or "poor man's caviar," is a spicy fish paste made from baby sardines and chili peppers. Spread it on bread or use it to add flavor to pasta.

### 3. Fileja Pasta

A traditional Calabrian pasta, fileja is hand-rolled and typically served with rich meat sauces or a simple spicy tomato sauce.

## 4. Tropea Onions

Sweet and mild, these red onions from Tropea are delicious raw in salads, caramelized in pasta, or pickled as a side dish.

## 5. Swordfish (Pesce Spada)

Swordfish is a popular seafood in Calabria, often grilled with lemon and olive oil or prepared as involtini (stuffed and rolled).

## 6. Stuffed Eggplant (Melanzane Ripiene)

Eggplant is a favorite in Calabria, and this dish features eggplants stuffed with breadcrumbs, cheese, garlic, and herbs, then baked until golden.

## 7. Pecorino Crotonese

A sheep's milk cheese from Crotone, pecorino crotonese can be enjoyed young and soft or aged and crumbly, often grated over pasta.

## 8. Pitta Calabrese

This traditional flatbread is stuffed with fillings like tomatoes, olives, and onions, or made sweet with nuts and raisins.

## 9. Lagane e Cicciari

An ancient pasta dish featuring wide noodles and chickpeas in a simple garlic, olive oil, and rosemary sauce, perfect for a comforting meal.

## 10. Tartufo di Pizzo

A delicious ice cream truffle from Pizzo, tartufo is made with layers of chocolate and hazelnut ice cream and has a melted chocolate center.

# Bars and Nightclubs

As you explore the towns and cities in this sunny region of southern Italy, you'll see that locals know how to have fun.

## Coastal Bars: A Key Part of Calabria's Nightlife

A great way to start your night in Calabria is by visiting its beautiful coastal towns. Places like

Tropea and Scilla have bars with stunning views of the Tyrrhenian Sea. In Tropea, many bars are hidden along charming streets that lead to the beach, offering a perfect mix of charm and atmosphere. Imagine sipping an Aperol Spritz or a glass of local Cirò wine while watching the sunset over the horizon—it's a classic Calabria experience.

In these bars, you'll often find the Italian tradition of aperitivo, where drinks come with light snacks like olives, bruschetta, and 'nduja sausage. Bars like Lido del Nonno and Caffè del Corso in Tropea are great spots to enjoy this social ritual.

If you're in Reggio Calabria, head to the Lungomare Falcomatà, known as "the most beautiful kilometer in Italy." This waterfront is lined with stylish bars, offering trendy cocktails and a view of Sicily in the distance. La Luna Ribelle is a popular spot for its creative drinks and chic vibe.

**Nightclubs: Where the Party Begins**
Calabria's nightclubs are full of energy,

especially in summer. In places like Soverato and Crotone, you'll find clubs that stay lively late into the night. Noa Club in Soverato is a famous outdoor nightclub on the beach, where you can dance under the stars with the sound of waves in the background. DJs here play a mix of electronic, house, and pop music, making sure everyone has a good time.

In Catanzaro, Atmosfera is a top club with modern decor and a great sound system. The music and dancing last until the early morning, and you'll be surrounded by stylish locals who love to party.

In Lamezia Terme, clubs like Room 21 offer a more laid-back vibe with live music and DJ sets, providing a fun night without the intensity of larger clubs.

## Live Music and Unique Venues

For something different, Calabria also has live music venues. The Roccella Jazz Festival is a famous summer event, but you can catch live performances throughout the year. In Reggio Calabria, Officina 52 is a popular spot for live music, from rock bands to acoustic sets. It's a cool place to enjoy good music while sipping on craft beers or cocktails.

# Traditional Japanese Dining Experiences

When you think of Calabria, Japanese food probably isn't the first thing that comes to mind. However, as global cultures mix with Italian cuisine, Calabria has developed its unique style of Japanese dining. As you travel through the region, you'll find Japanese dining experiences blending beautifully with the local flavors of southern Italy, creating a unique culinary adventure.

### Sushi in Calabria

You might not expect to find a sushi bar in a small Calabrian town, but Calabria's love for fresh ingredients makes it a great fit for sushi-making. With access to plenty of fresh seafood, Calabria offers sushi that can rival that of bigger cities. Whether you're in the bustling Reggio Calabria or a quiet coastal village, you'll find sushi restaurants serving expertly crafted nigiri, sashimi, and maki rolls.

These sushi spots often have a minimalist Japanese feel, with simple décor and bamboo accents. Many chefs are trained in Japan or by Japanese masters, blending fresh local fish with traditional sushi-making techniques. The combination of sushi's delicate flavors and Calabria's bold wines makes for a memorable meal.

## Teppanyaki: A Fusion of Japanese and Italian Hospitality

Teppanyaki restaurants are another exciting part of Calabria's Japanese dining scene. In these places, dining is also a show, with chefs cooking on a flat grill right in front of you. The chefs often use local ingredients like Calabrian beef or fresh Mediterranean seafood, adding an Italian touch to the traditional Japanese teppanyaki experience.

Imagine enjoying a perfectly grilled slice of swordfish or tender local beef, cooked with precision but flavored with Calabrian spices and olive oil. This blend of Japanese cooking methods and Italian flavors creates a one-of-a-kind dining experience.

## Kaiseki: A Japanese Multi-Course Experience

For a more formal Japanese meal, Calabria offers kaiseki dining, where you enjoy a multi-course meal featuring seasonal ingredients. Each dish is carefully crafted to showcase balance and artistry, and local Calabrian ingredients like fresh herbs, tomatoes, and citrus are often incorporated into the courses.

One highlight is the use of local fish like sea bream or tuna, cooked in traditional Japanese styles with a Mediterranean twist, such as a drizzle of olive oil or a sprinkle of basil. Kaiseki dining in Calabria is a beautiful blend of Japanese elegance and southern Italian flavors.

## Japanese Tea Ceremonies with a Calabrian Twist

Some restaurants in Calabria also offer traditional Japanese tea ceremonies, giving you a taste of Japan's ancient tea culture. What makes it special here is the addition of locally grown herbs, alongside traditional matcha. The ceremony, combined with Calabrian warmth and hospitality, creates a peaceful, cross-cultural experience you won't forget.

## Dining Recommendations

### Budget Friendly Dining

Here are three great places to eat in Calabria that offer good food at reasonable prices, along with their locations, best dishes, atmosphere, contact info, and opening hours.

**1. La Tavernetta**

 La Tavernetta is a cozy, family-owned restaurant offering traditional Calabrian food at affordable prices. They are known for homemade pasta and fresh seafood.

*Location:* Contrada Pietrastorta, 45, 89126, Reggio Calabria Italy

*Phone:* +39 0965 318051

## Hours:

Sun: 12:30 PM - 3:00 PM, 7:30 PM - 10:30 PM
Mon: 7:30 PM - 10:30 PM
Tue: 7:45 PM - 10:30 PM
Wed: 7:45 PM - 10:30 PM
Thu: 12:30 PM - 2:30 PM, 7:45 PM - 10:30 PM
Fri: 7:45 PM - 10:30 PM
Sat: 12:30 PM - 2:30 PM, 8:00 PM - 11:00 PM

## Must-Try Dishes:

- Spaghetti with clams (€10)
- Fried squid (€12)
- Tiramisu (€5)

## Atmosphere:

Simple and homey, with wooden tables and vintage photos of Calabria. It feels like dining in a local home with friendly service.

## 2. Trattoria del Pesce Fresco

 This restaurant sits by the sea in Tropea and specializes in fresh, affordable seafood. It's a great spot to enjoy a meal with ocean views.

*Location:* Via Fratelli Cairoli 7, 89127, Reggio Calabria Italy

*Phone:* +39 346 402 0817

*Hours:*
Mon: 11:00 AM - 3:00 PM, 7:00 PM - 11:59 PM
Tue: 11:00 AM - 3:00 PM, 7:00 PM - 11:59 PM
Wed: 11:00 AM - 3:00 PM, 7:00 PM - 11:59 PM
Thu: 11:00 AM - 3:00 PM, 7:00 PM - 11:59 PM
Fri: 11:00 AM - 3:00 PM, 7:00 PM - 11:59 PM
Sat: 11:00 AM - 3:00 PM, 7:00 PM - 11:59 PM

*Must-Try Dishes:*
- Linguine with pistachio pesto and shrimp (€11)
- Grilled swordfish (€14)
- Spicy Calabrian sausage-flavored ice cream (€4)

*Atmosphere:*
Relaxed and casual, with outdoor seating and views of the Tyrrhenian Sea. Decorated with fishing nets, it has a laid-back, beach vibe.

### 3. Da Mario 1976 Ristorante Pizzeria Bar

Da Mario is a classic eatery in the historic town of Corigliano Calabro. It's known for serving filling, traditional Calabrian dishes at low prices.

*Location:* Via Nazionale 13, 87070 Roseto Capo Spulico Italy

*Phone:* +39 388 182 3014

*Hours:*
Sun: 12:00 AM - 11:59 PM
Mon: 12:00 AM - 11:59 PM
Tue: 12:00 AM - 11:59 PM
Wed: 12:00 AM - 11:59 PM
Thu: 12:00 AM - 11:59 PM
Fri: 12:00 AM - 11:59 PM
Sat: 12:00 AM - 11:59 PM

*Must-Try Dishes:*
• Potato gnocchi with basil pesto (€8)

- Eggplant meatballs (€9)
- Panna cotta (€4)

*Atmosphere:*
Rustic and welcoming, with terracotta floors and wooden beams. A great place to enjoy a relaxed, family-style meal.

## Mid Range Dining

Here's a simple overview of three mid-range restaurants in Calabria, each offering a unique taste of the region's food.

### 1. Ristorante La Pentola d'Oro

 This coastal restaurant is a short walk from the ferry terminal to Sicily and serves authentic Calabrian seafood and Italian dishes.

*Location:* Via Pelliccia Snc, 89861 Tropea Italy

*Phone:* +39 0963 607073

*Menu Highlights:*

- Grilled Swordfish
- Spaghetti with clams and bottarga
- 'Nduja pizza
- Mixed seafood platter

*Ambiance:*

A cozy, family-friendly spot with sea views and outdoor seating.

*Hours:*

Sun: 12:00 PM - 3:00 PM, 7:00 PM - 12:00 AM

Mon: 12:00 PM - 3:00 PM, 7:00 PM - 12:00 AM

Tue: 12:00 PM - 3:00 PM, 7:00 PM - 12:00 AM

Wed: 12:00 PM - 3:00 PM, 7:00 PM - 12:00 AM

Thu: 12:00 PM - 3:00 PM, 7:00 PM - 12:00 AM

Fri: 12:00 PM - 3:00 PM, 7:00 PM - 12:00 AM

Sat: 12:00 PM - 3:00 PM, 7:00 PM - 12:00 AM

## 2. Osteria il Brigante

A charming spot offering hearty Calabrian dishes, including seafood and inland specialties.

*Location:* C.DA DIFISELLA, 88836, Cotronei
Italy

*Phone:* +39 0962 491979

*Menu Highlights:*
- Eggplant Parmigiana
- Pasta alla Sila (mushrooms and sausage)
- Grilled fresh fish
- Slow-cooked lamb

*Ambiance:*
Rustic and cozy with exposed brick and wooden beams.

*Hours:*
12:30 PM - 3:00 PM, 7:30 PM - 11:00 PM (Closed Tuesdays)

### 3. Il Cantagalli

A lively restaurant in Lamezia Terme offering a mix of regional and Italian dishes, known for its pizza and pasta.

*Location:* Via San Rocco 19, 88046 Lamezia Terme Italy

*Phone:* +39 0968 441738

*Menu Highlights:*
- Calabrese pizza with 'nduja and olives
- Truffle pasta
- Veal Milanese
- Seafood risotto

*Ambiance:*
Trendy and vibrant with a modern, comfortable interior.

*Hours:*
12:00 PM - 3:00 PM, 7:00 PM - 11:30 PM (Open every day)

# Luxurious Dining

### 1. Le Quattro Fontane – Tropea

*Location:* Largo Mercato 22, 89861 Tropea Italy

*Phone:* +39 324 098 8746

*Hours:*

Sun: 12:00 PM - 3:00 PM, 7:00 PM - 10:30 PM

Mon: 7:00 PM - 10:30 PM

Tue: 12:00 PM - 3:00 PM, 7:00 PM - 10:30 PM

Wed: 12:00 PM - 3:00 PM, 7:00 PM - 10:30 PM

Thu: 12:00 PM - 3:00 PM, 7:00 PM - 10:30 PM

Fri: 12:00 PM - 3:00 PM, 7:00 PM - 10:30 PM

Sat: 12:00 PM - 3:00 PM, 7:00 PM - 10:30 PM

*Menu:*

This upscale restaurant in Tropea offers traditional Calabrian dishes with a gourmet twist, especially seafood. Popular choices include Gnocchi al Pesto di Pistacchio (gnocchi with pistachio pesto) and Tonno alla Tropeana (tuna with local onions). Don't miss the house-made Tartufo di Pizzo for dessert.

*Ambiance:*

Set in an 18th-century building, the restaurant blends elegance and comfort. You can enjoy a meal on the outdoor terrace with views of the sea and Tropea's old town, perfect for a romantic evening or special occasion.

## 2. La Locanda di Alia – Castrovillari

*Location:* Via Ietticelli 55, 87012 Castrovillari Italy

*Phone:* +39 0981 46370

*Hours:*

Sun: 1:00 PM - 3:00 PM

Mon: 8:00 PM - 10:00 PM

Tue: 1:00 PM - 3:00 PM, 8:00 PM - 10:00 PM

Wed: 1:00 PM - 3:00 PM, 8:00 PM - 10:00 PM

Thu: 1:00 PM - 3:00 PM, 8:00 PM - 10:00 PM

Fri: 1:00 PM - 3:00 PM, 8:00 PM - 10:00 PM

Sat: 1:00 PM - 3:00 PM, 8:00 PM - 10:00 PM

*Menu:*

This family-run restaurant offers a creative take on traditional Calabrian cuisine, featuring dishes like Fusilli con Ragù di Maialino Nero (pasta with black pig ragout) and Filetto di Manzo al Bergamotto (beef with bergamot glaze). The wine list includes rare Calabrian wines.

*Ambiance:*

The restaurant has a cozy, rustic feel, with vintage decor and an outdoor terrace surrounded by greenery. It's perfect for a quiet, elegant meal in a peaceful setting.

### 3. Il Castello di Serragiumenta – Altomonte

*Location:* Piazza Castello 6, 87042 Altomonte Italy

*Phone:* +39 0981 948933

## Hours:

Tuesday to Sunday: 12:30 PM - 3:00 PM, 7:30 PM - 11:00 PM (Closed Mondays)

## Menu:

Located in a restored castle, this restaurant focuses on traditional Calabrian food, with an emphasis on meat dishes like Agnello alla Griglia (grilled lamb) and Tagliata di Manzo (sliced beef). The sommelier ensures perfect wine pairings with each dish.

## Ambiance:

Dining in a castle offers a truly luxurious experience. You can eat in the grand halls or on the terrace overlooking the beautiful Altamonte hills, making this an unforgettable dining experience.

# Chapter 5

# Outdoor Activities in Calabria

## Skiing and Snowboarding

Calabria has two main mountain ranges which are the Aspromonte and the Sila, both are perfect for winter sports, with beautiful scenery and well-developed facilities.

### Sila National Park: Calabria's Skiing Hub

The Sila Mountain Range, part of Sila National Park, is the center of skiing and snowboarding in Calabria. From December to March, this area becomes a winter wonderland with slopes for beginners and advanced skiers alike.

The main ski resort in this region is Camigliatello Silano, located at 1,400 meters. It offers multiple ski runs, a snow park for snowboarders and freestyle skiers, and lifts to suit all skill levels. Beginners and families will find easy slopes, while advanced skiers can take on the steeper runs.

Another popular resort is Lorica, which boasts stunning views of Lake Arvo and the surrounding mountains. It has several ski trails, modern lifts, and a snow park, with snowmaking machines ensuring good snow conditions all season long.

### Aspromonte Mountains: Skiing by the Sea

In the Aspromonte Mountains, **Gambarie Ski Resort** offers a unique experience with views of the sea from its slopes. Located near Reggio Calabria, the resort sits at over 1,300 meters and features ski lifts, snowmaking equipment, and slopes for different skill levels. Here, you can ski in the morning and visit the beach in the afternoon—a rare combination that attracts many visitors.

# Hiking and Nature Trails

Calabria, located between the Ionian and Tyrrhenian Seas, is a great destination for nature lovers. It offers many hiking trails with amazing views, rich wildlife, and a sense of history. The region's rugged mountains, green forests, and beautiful coastlines make it perfect for outdoor adventures.

## Aspromonte National Park

Aspromonte National Park is one of Calabria's top spots for hikers. Found in the southern part of the region, it features stunning mountain views, thick forests, and rare plants and animals. The highest point, Montalto, has trails for all skill levels, with panoramic views of both the Ionian and Tyrrhenian Seas. A well-known trail, the "Sentiero Italia" (Italy Trail), crosses through the park, leading hikers past old villages, rivers, and deep gorges. The park also features the impressive Cascade Maesano waterfalls, which are a must-see.

## Sila National Park

Sila National Park, located in central Calabria, is often called the region's "Green Lung." Unlike Aspromonte, it has rolling hills, peaceful lakes, and large forests of pine and beech trees. It's great for both easy walks and challenging hikes. Trails like "Camigliatello – Monte Curcio" provide calm views of Lake Cecita, and you might even spot wolves, deer, or eagles. In winter, many trails are used for cross-country skiing.

## Coastal Hiking in Tropea and Capo Vaticano

If you prefer hiking along the coast, the area around Tropea and Capo Vaticano offers scenic walks along cliffs with views of clear blue water. The popular "Sentiero del Tracciolino" trail follows the coastline, passing fishing villages, vineyards, and lemon trees. You'll enjoy beautiful views of the Tyrrhenian Sea, and on clear days, you can even see the Aeolian Islands.

## Gerace and Stilo

For a mix of history and nature, the medieval towns of Gerace and Stilo are surrounded by scenic trails. The "Gerace Loop" takes you through old olive groves with views of the mountains and the sea. The "Stilo Cattolica" trail leads past the famous Byzantine church and into the hills of Aspromonte.

# Diving and Snorkeling Spots

Calabria's beautiful coastline is home to some of Italy's best spots for diving and snorkeling. Let's take a look at some of the top snorkeling and diving spots in Calabria:'

## Top Snorkeling Spots

1. *Capo Vaticano:* This famous headland on the Tyrrhenian Sea is ideal for snorkeling. Its shallow waters are full of colorful fish, sea urchins, and octopuses. The clear water around Grotticelle Beach lets you see the vibrant underwater life easily.

2. *Spiaggia di Caminia:* Located on the Ionian coast, Caminia Beach is known for its calm waters and rocky seabed. The clear waters reveal schools of fish and interesting rock formations. The beach is set in a scenic cove surrounded by cliffs, perfect for exploring marine life up close.

3. *Scilla:* Famous from mythology, Scilla's waters are beautiful and safe for snorkeling. The beach has rock formations and underwater

caves where you can find small fish, crabs, and sea anemones.

**Top Diving Spots**

1. *Tropea:* With its dramatic cliffs and turquoise waters, Tropea offers excellent diving. You can explore underwater caves and steep walls that are home to sea turtles, moray eels, and colorful corals. The Sanctuary of Santa Maria dell'Isola adds a stunning view above and below the water.

2. *Capo Rizzuto Marine Reserve:* This protected area on the Ionian coast is a diver's dream. It features well-preserved reefs, underwater archaeological sites, and a wide range of marine life including groupers, amberjacks, and rays. You can also see remnants of shipwrecks here.

3. *Pizzo Calabro:* Known for its blue waters, Pizzo Calabro offers interesting underwater caves and tunnels. The dive sites are full of sponges, barracudas, and sea fans. The calm waters make it a great spot for beginner divers.

# Fishing and Water Activities

Fishing is a beloved tradition in Calabria, deeply ingrained in the local culture. The clear waters and abundant marine life make it a great spot for all levels of anglers. Coastal towns like Tropea and Scilla are perfect for shore fishing, offering beautiful seaside views. For a more adventurous experience, you can join deep-sea fishing trips from ports like Reggio Calabria or Lamezia Terme, where you can catch big fish like tuna and marlin while enjoying the stunning Calabrian coastline.

If you prefer a quieter fishing experience, the lakes in Sila National Park offer peaceful settings for fly fishing. The beautiful landscapes, with forests and rolling hills, provide a serene backdrop for a day on the water.

Calabria's waters are also great for other activities. Scuba diving and snorkeling reveal a vibrant underwater world, especially around Capo Vaticano and the Aeolian Islands, known for their clear waters, colorful fish, ancient shipwrecks, and interesting rock formations.

Whether you're an experienced diver or a beginner, there's something for everyone.

Kayaking and paddleboarding are popular too, letting you explore the coastline at a leisurely pace. The calm waters and hidden beaches of places like the Gulf of Squillace and the area near Praia a Mare are perfect for these activities, offering a relaxing way to enjoy Calabria's beautiful coastline.

## Best Beaches in Calabria

If you want to relax and have a fun time, you can visit these beaches in Calabria:

### Tropea Beach: A Tyrrhenian Gem

Tropea Beach is the most well-known in Calabria, featuring clear turquoise waters and soft, golden sand. It's located beneath high cliffs, with the charming town of Tropea perched above. One of the highlights is the view

 of the Sanctuary of Santa Maria dell'Isola, a church that sits on a rocky outcrop over the sea. Tropea Beach is great for

swimming, sunbathing, and snorkeling, offering both excitement and relaxation.

**Capo Vaticano: Calabria's Tropical Escape**
Capo Vaticano, close to Tropea, is considered one of Italy's most stunning beaches. It has  white sandy shores and dramatic rock formations that give it a tropical feel. The water is crystal clear, perfect for snorkeling and diving. The cliffs offer amazing views of the Aeolian Islands, making it a top spot for adventure and natural beauty.

**Spiaggia di Caminia: A Quiet Retreat**
Spiaggia di Caminia, on the Ionian Coast, is a hidden treasure for those seeking a quieter beach experience. Tucked between steep cliffs, the beach has clear waters and smooth pebbles,  making it ideal for swimming and relaxing. The rocky surroundings are perfect for exploring, and the calm waters are great for snorkeling. Despite its peacefulness, the beach has basic facilities, so it's easy to visit.

**Grotticelle Beach: A Diver's Paradise**

Grotticelle Beach, near Capo Vaticano, is a favorite for divers and  snorkelers. Its waters are full of vibrant marine life and interesting underwater rock formations. With soft sand and shallow waters, the beach is also family-friendly, offering fun for adventurers and beachgoers alike.

# Top 5 Annual Events and Festivals to Attend

Here are five popular festivals worth attending in the region.

## 1. Tarantella Power Festival (Caulonia)

Held every August, the Tarantella Power Festival in Caulonia celebrates the traditional Southern Italian folk dance, the tarantella. This energetic event brings musicians, dancers, and performers together to showcase the dance, believed to have ancient healing powers.

Visitors can enjoy live music, free dance workshops, and sample local crafts and cuisine.

## 2. Sagra della Cipolla Rossa (Tropea)

The Red Onion Festival in Tropea, held in late July, celebrates the famous Tropea red onion with cooking demonstrations, tastings, and dishes featuring this special ingredient. The festival offers food lovers a chance to explore Calabria's rich culinary traditions with live music and entertainment.

## 3. Festa di San Francesco di Paola (Paola)

Every May in Paola, the Festa di San Francesco di Paola honors Calabria's patron saint with religious processions, prayers, and a reenactment of his sea voyage. The festival includes a lively street market, music, and fireworks, making it a meaningful experience for those interested in Calabria's religious heritage.

## 4. Palio di Ribusa (Cosenza)

The Palio di Ribusa is a medieval-themed festival held in September in Cosenza, where the city transforms into a medieval village. The event features jousting, parades, and a traditional horse race, offering visitors a chance to step back in time and experience the history of Cosenza.

### 5. Peperoncino Festival (Diamante)

The Peperoncino Festival in Diamante, held every September, celebrates Calabria's love for spicy food. The festival features cooking demonstrations, spicy eating contests, and vendors selling chili-infused products. It's a fun, fiery event that showcases Calabria's bold flavors and culinary passion.

# Chapter 6

# Accommodation Options in Calabria

## Budget Friendly Stays

If you're traveling on a budget, there are plenty of affordable hotels that offer great value without sacrificing comfort. Here are three budget-friendly hotels in Calabria, along with details on their amenities, locations, and check-in/check-out times.

### 1. Hotel Medinblu

Hotel Medinblu is a great choice for budget travelers in Reggio Calabria. It offers modern comforts and a friendly atmosphere, and it is located near the famous Lungomare promenade with amazing views of the Messina Strait. At the hotel, every room has a wardrobe.

 Each room also has a private bathroom with free toiletries, a flat-screen TV, and air conditioning, and some rooms

have a balcony. Every room comes with a desk and a kettle. Breakfast is served every morning with buffet, continental, and Italian options available. It's perfect for those who want to explore the city without spending too much.

*Location:* Via Demetrio Tripepi 98, 89125 Reggio Calabria, Italy

*Price Range:* $80 - $100 per night

*Amenities:*
- Free Wi-Fi
- Complimentary breakfast
- Rooftop terrace with views
- Air-conditioned rooms with private bathrooms
- Laundry service
- 24-hour front desk
- Family rooms available

*Check-in/Check-out:*
- Check-in: From 2:00 PM
- Check-out: By 10:30 AM

## 2. Il Borgo della Marinella

Located in the peaceful town of Falerna, Il Borgo della Marinella is a quiet retreat by the sea. With its rustic charm and lovely gardens, this family-run hotel offers a relaxing stay without breaking the bank. Designed to  resemble a traditional farm village, Il Borgo Della Marinella combines old-world charm with modern comforts. Completely renovated in 2005, it is located in a valley 30 meters above sea level, just 400 meters from the beach.

*Location:* Formiciche,35 c.da marinella Oliva, 87032 Campora San Giovanni Italy

*Price Range:* $70 - $90 per night

*Amenities:*
- Free Parking
- Swimming pool with sun loungers
- Restaurant with local cuisine
- Free Wi-Fi
- Air-conditioned rooms with flat-screen

TVs
- Private balconies in select rooms
- Shuttle service to nearby spots

### *Check-in/Check-out:*
- Check-in: From 3:00 PM
- Check-out: By 11:00 AM

### 3. Hotel Conte Ruggero

Hotel Conte Ruggero is located in the mountains of Serra San Bruno, offering a quiet and scenic escape for nature  lovers. The rooms at Conte Ruggero Hotel come with a balcony, minibar, and a cooling fan. Each room has its bathroom with free toiletries and a hairdryer. Soverato, known for its sandy beaches, is 35 km from the hotel. Pizzo can be reached in a 40-minute drive. This budget hotel is perfect for hikers and those looking to explore Calabria's inland beauty.

*Location:* Piazza Tenente Bruno Pisani, 1, 89822 Serra San Bruno, Italy

***Price Range:*** $50 - $75 per night

***Amenities:***
- Free Wi-Fi
- Traditional breakfast included
- Pet-friendly
- Cozy rooms with air conditioning and private bathrooms
- Flat-screen TVs
- Free Parking
- Laundry service

***Check-in/Check-out:***
- Check-in: From 12:00 PM
- Check-out: By 10:30 AM

# Mid Range Hotels

## 1. Hotel Ristorante La Bussola, Capo Vaticano

***Location:*** Via G. Berto, 89865 Capo Vaticano, Italy

Hotel Ristorante La Bussola is great for families

and beachgoers. Located in Capo Vaticano, just 900 meters from the beach, La Bussola Hotel has a large garden with a swimming pool and free parking. Every room includes a private balcony and free Wi-Fi. The rooms at La Bussola Hotel Calabria are air-conditioned and come with a minibar and satellite TV. Some rooms have views of the garden, while others offer sea views.

*Amenities:*

- Air-conditioned rooms with satellite TV and private balconies
- Free Wi-Fi
- Outdoor pool with children's area
- Free breakfast buffet
- Restaurant serving seafood and local dishes
- Shuttle to nearby beaches
- Free Parking
- Garden with loungers and umbrellas
- Bar and terrace

*Check-in/Check-out:*

- Check-in: 3:00 PM
- Check-out: 10:30 AM

## 2. Hotel San Francesco, Rende (Cosenza)

*Location:* Via Ungaretti 2, 87036 Rende, Italy

Located in Rende, near Cosenza, Hotel San Francesco is a modern hotel suitable for both leisure and business travelers.  Hotel San Francesco is in Rende, in Cosenza's new business and shopping area. The rooms have free Wi-Fi and Sky Gold TV channels, including sports. The Tyrrhenian Sea and Sila Mountains are about a 20-minute drive away. The hotel's restaurant offers traditional Calabrian dishes and some national favorites. Breakfast features a variety of fresh items.

*Amenities:*
- Air-conditioned rooms with flat-screen TVs, mini-bars, and private bathrooms
- Free Wi-Fi
- Restaurant serving local and Italian dishes

- Free breakfast buffet
- Fitness center
- Meeting rooms
- Free Parking
- 24-hour front desk
- Bar and coffee lounge

### *Check-in/Check-out:*
- Check-in: 2:00 PM
- Check-out: 11:00 AM

### 3. Il Borghetto Creative Resort, Gerace

*Location:* Viale Don Mottola c/o Grafiche Romano s.r.l., 89861 Tropea, Italy

Il Borghetto Creative Resort is in the historic  town of Gerace, perfect for travelers interested in culture and history. It is a 4-star hotel in Tropea, located 1.9 km from Lido Alex. It offers accommodation with a seasonal outdoor pool, free private parking, a garden, and a terrace. The hotel provides free WiFi and has a bar. Some rooms even have a patio with a sea view.

Each room at the hotel has a desk, air conditioning, and a flat-screen TV. All rooms come with a private bathroom, including a bidet and free toiletries. Some rooms also have a balcony. For added security, rooms are equipped with a safe.

*Amenities:*
- Elegant, air-conditioned rooms with hill views
- Free Wi-Fi
- Free continental breakfast
- Outdoor terrace with panoramic views
- Restaurant using local, seasonal ingredients
- Gardens for relaxing
- Private parking
- Library and reading room
- Free bicycle rentals

*Check-in/Check-out:*
- Check-in: 3:00 PM
- Check-out: 11:00 AM

## Luxurious Hotels

Here's a detailed look at three luxurious hotels

in Calabria, including what they offer, their locations, and check-in and check-out times. Each hotel provides unique experiences for travelers seeking comfort, elegance, and excellent service.

## 1. Capovaticano Resort Thalasso & Spa

*Location:* Località Tono - Frazione San Nicolò, 89866 Capo Vaticano, Italy

This resort is located on the beautiful Capo Vaticano coastline, offering stunning views of  the Tyrrhenian Sea and Aeolian Islands. Capovaticano Resort Thalasso and Spa has bright, modern rooms with flat-screen TVs and satellite channels. Each room offers views of the gardens or the sea, and some rooms have a large balcony or terrace.

Inside, guests can unwind in the spa, which offers thalassotherapy treatments, massages, and a hot tub. Outside, there are water sports like sailing, windsurfing, and diving available for guests to enjoy. It's perfect for a luxurious beach getaway with wellness treatments.

*Amenities:*
- Private beach with clear waters and sunbeds
- Spa with sea-based treatments
- Indoor and outdoor pools
- Multiple dining options, including Mediterranean dishes and seafood
- Modern fitness center
- Water sports: windsurfing, sailing, snorkeling
- Rooms with sea-view terraces and stylish furnishings

*Check-in/Check-out:*
- Check-in: 3:00 PM
- Check-out: 12:00 PM

## 2. Palazzo Marzano

*Location:* Corso Regina Margherita, 89817 Briatico Italy

Housed in an 18th-century palace, this boutique

hotel mixes historic charm with modern luxury, offering a calm and elegant atmosphere near the coast. At the hotel, every room has a desk. All

rooms at Palazzo Marzano have a private bathroom with free toiletries, a flat-screen TV, and air conditioning. Some rooms also have a balcony. Every room includes a wardrobe.

Capo Vaticano Lighthouse is 26 km away, and the nearest airport, Lamezia Terme International Airport, is 44 km from Palazzo Marzano.

*Amenities:*

- Spacious rooms with antique décor and modern touches
- Fine-dining restaurant serving Calabrian and international cuisine
- Courtyard and garden for outdoor dining
- Private beach access (a short drive away)
- Personalized concierge services
- Free Wi-Fi
- In-room spa services

## Check-in/Check-out:

- Check-in: 2:00 PM
- Check-out: 11:00 AM

## 3. Villa Paola

*Location:* Contrada Paola, 89861 Tropea (VV)

Located in Tropea, this luxury boutique hotel offers a peaceful retreat with fantastic sea views. Villa Paola, located in a 16th-century convent, has an outdoor pool, a sun terrace, and  a garden. The stylish rooms come with flat-screen satellite TVs and are 1.5 km from Tropea. The villa is surrounded by a large garden and sun terrace, with the pool offering stunning views of the Tyrrhenian Sea.

Each soundproof room has a private bathroom with a bathrobe and free toiletries. Free Wi-Fi is available throughout the property. Every morning, a breakfast buffet is served with homemade pastries, fruit juices, and cappuccino coffee.

## *Amenities:*

- An infinity pool with ocean views
- Beautiful gardens with lounge areas
- Gourmet restaurant serving local dishes
- Stylish rooms with sea views and private terraces
- Concierge services for boat tours and cultural excursions
- Free breakfast served in the garden or terrace
- Shuttle service to Tropea's beach and town center

## *Check-in/Check-out:*

- Check-in: 3:00 PM
- Check-out: 11:00 AM

# Chapter 7
# Practical Information
## Shopping in Calabria

Calabria, the southernmost part of mainland Italy, is famous for its stunning landscapes and rich history, but it also boasts a lively shopping scene. Whether you live there or are just visiting, exploring the markets, artisan shops, and boutiques in Calabria is a delightful experience filled with local flavors, traditional crafts, and unique souvenirs.

**Local Markets**

A great way to dive into Calabrian culture is by visiting local markets. These lively spots are brimming with fresh produce, regional specialties, and handmade goods. Notable markets can be found in towns like Reggio Calabria, Cosenza, and Catanzaro.

In Reggio Calabria, the Piazza Camagna market is bustling in the mornings with vendors selling vibrant fruits, local cheeses, and cured meats. Be sure to try 'nduja, a spicy, spreadable salami that's a Calabrian specialty.

Cosenza's Mercato di Corso Mazzini is another must-see, offering local crafts, textiles, and artisanal products alongside fresh food. It's a great place to meet local artisans and farmers and learn about the region's culinary and craft traditions.

**Artisan Shops**

Calabria has a strong tradition of artisanal craftsmanship. Many towns feature small workshops where skilled artisans create beautiful handmade items. In Tropea, known for its stunning cliffs and beaches, you'll find shops specializing in ceramics and woven goods. The local pottery often features traditional designs and bright colors, making them perfect souvenirs.

In Gerace, you can explore artisan shops offering intricate wooden carvings, handmade jewelry, and textiles. These items reflect the local culture and history, making them unique mementos of your visit. Buying these products supports local artisans and gives you a special piece of Calabria to take home.

## Boutiques and Fashion

Calabria's shopping scene also includes modern boutiques and fashion shops that cater to various tastes. Cities offer a mix of local and international brands, providing stylish clothing, accessories, and footwear. Catanzaro is known for its shoe shops, where you can find beautifully crafted leather shoes that are both stylish and comfortable.

For something unique, visit Via Giuseppe Garibaldi in Reggio Calabria, where chic boutiques offer everything from elegant clothing to handcrafted accessories. Many shops focus on sustainable fashion, featuring eco-friendly materials that support local artisans.

## Local Products and Gourmet Shops

Food lovers will find plenty to enjoy in Calabria. Gourmet shops, known as "alimentari," specialize in local products like olive oil, wine, and preserves. Look for shops that offer tastings, where you can sample famous Cirò wine or the sweet red onions of Tropea.

Sila National Park also produces high-quality honey, cheeses, and cured meats, available in specialty stores throughout the region. These products make great gifts for food enthusiasts and a tasty way to bring a piece of Calabria home.

## Souvenir Shopping

For souvenirs, Calabria offers a range of options that capture the region's essence. Popular choices include ceramic tiles with traditional motifs, handmade lace, and locally crafted jewelry. 'Nduja and other local delicacies also make excellent edible souvenirs.

For a cultural touch, consider Calabrian books or art prints depicting local landscapes and heritage. These make unique decorative pieces and great conversation starters about your travels.

# Health and Medical Services

Calabria's healthcare is part of Italy's national health service, Servizio Sanitario Nazionale (SSN). This system offers public healthcare that is mostly free or low-cost for Italian residents. Visitors should have travel insurance or a European Health Insurance Card (EHIC) if they're from the EU, as this can help with medical costs.

## Hospitals and Medical Facilities

Calabria has several well-regarded hospitals and medical centers in its major cities and towns:

- *Reggio Calabria:* Policlinico Universitario Giaccone* is a major hospital with comprehensive services, including emergency care and specialist consultations. It's affiliated with the University of Reggio Calabria, ensuring high-quality care.
- *Cosenza:* Ospedale dell'Annunziata offers a range of services from general medicine to specialized treatments and has a well-equipped emergency

department.

- *Catanzaro:* Pugliese-Ciaccio Hospital is known for its modern facilities and specialties like cardiology and orthopedics.

Smaller clinics and health centers throughout Calabria provide primary care, dental services, and other routine medical needs.

**Pharmacies**

Pharmacies are common in Calabria and are usually marked with a green cross. They offer over-the-counter and prescription medications. Most pharmacists speak basic English, but knowing some Italian phrases can be helpful. A doctor's prescription is needed for prescription medications, which can be obtained from local healthcare providers.

**Emergency Services**

For emergencies, dial 112, the national emergency number available throughout Calabria. This connects you to medical, fire, and police services. Hospitals and emergency rooms are ready to handle urgent care, so it's a good idea to know the nearest hospital to your location.

**Travel Health Tips**

Travelers should keep a few health tips in mind when visiting Calabria:

- *Vaccinations:* Ensure routine vaccinations are up-to-date. No special vaccines are needed for Calabria, but standard health precautions are recommended.
- *Sun Protection:* Calabria has a Mediterranean climate with hot summers. Use sun protection to avoid sunburn and dehydration.
- *Food and Water Safety:* Tap water is generally safe to drink, but bottled water is available if you have a sensitive stomach. Enjoy local food but be cautious with street food to avoid stomach issues.

**Health Insurance and Medical Costs**

Travel insurance is strongly recommended to cover medical expenses. EU citizens can use the EHIC for reduced-cost state healthcare services. Non-EU travelers should ensure their insurance covers medical emergencies and hospital stays.

# Internet and Wi-Fi Access

If you're visiting Calabria, staying connected is important, but internet access might not be as advanced as in bigger cities like Rome or Milan. The internet in Calabria can be slower, especially in rural areas. However, improvements are being made to increase availability for tourists.

**Wi-Fi in Cities and Towns**

In larger cities like Reggio Calabria, Catanzaro, and Cosenza, Wi-Fi is available in public areas, hotels, cafes, and restaurants. Most hotels offer free Wi-Fi, though speeds may vary. Many restaurants and cafes also provide free Wi-Fi for guests.

In more remote areas or rural accommodations

like farm stays (agriturismos), internet access may be slower or less reliable. It's a good idea to check with your hotel about Wi-Fi availability when booking.

Public Wi-Fi hotspots are also common in popular tourist areas, like parks and piazzas. For example, Reggio Calabria has public Wi-Fi along the Lungomare Falcomatà, a scenic seafront promenade.

**Mobile Internet and 4G/5G Networks**

For constant internet access, using mobile data is often the best option. Major Italian providers like TIM, Vodafone, and WindTre offer 4G coverage in most towns and some 5G in larger cities like Reggio Calabria and Cosenza.

If you need a lot of data for navigation or communication, you might want to buy a local SIM card. Tourist data plans are available at airports and stores, often offering between 10GB to 50GB of data at affordable rates.

In more remote areas, such as national parks,

mobile coverage can be patchy. It's a good idea to download maps or guides for offline use if you're heading into these areas.

## Internet in Rural and Coastal Areas

While rural areas of Calabria offer stunning views, internet access may be slower. Coastal towns like Tropea and Scilla generally have better connectivity, with many hotels and beach clubs offering Wi-Fi. In smaller villages or mountainous areas, the internet might be less reliable, though the government is working on improving rural access with fiber-optic networks.

## Tips for Staying Connected in Calabria

- *Be cautious with public Wi-Fi:* To protect your data, use a VPN when connecting to public Wi-Fi networks.
- *Download maps and guides:* In case of spotty coverage in rural areas, it's smart to download essential information before your trip.
- *Local SIM cards:* These are usually cheaper than international roaming, and mobile providers often offer plans with

good coverage and English-language support.

## Local Customs and Etiquette

Here's a simple guide to the key customs and etiquette in Calabria.

### Family Life

In Calabria, family is at the heart of daily life. Families are often large and close-knit, and it's common for several generations to live together. Family gatherings, and huge meals, are a central part of social life, and Sundays are typically reserved for long family lunches.

If you're invited to a family meal, consider it an honor. Be ready for a long, delicious meal, and be sure to compliment the food and thank your hosts. Bringing a small gift, like wine or dessert, is also appreciated.

### Greetings and Social Customs

Greetings in Calabria are warm and friendly. People often greet each other with a kiss on both cheeks, whether they are men or women. However, in formal settings like business meetings, a handshake may be more appropriate. When entering or leaving a shop or cafe, it's polite to say "Buongiorno" (Good morning), "Buonasera" (Good evening), "Grazie" (Thank you), or "Arrivederci" (Goodbye).

Eye contact is important in conversations, as it shows sincerity. Calabrians, like many Italians, use hand gestures when they talk. Don't be surprised if locals strike up friendly conversations with you, and they will appreciate it if you show interest in their culture.

## Dining Etiquette

Meals in Calabria are leisurely and social. They often include several courses, such as appetizers, pasta, meat or fish, and desserts. Meals are to be enjoyed slowly, so don't rush. Bread is often served, but don't eat it before the meal starts, or use it to clean your plate until you're almost done.

It's polite to wait until everyone has been served before you start eating. If wine is served, a toast of "Salute!" may be made before the first sip. If you are a guest in someone's home, offer to help clear the table, but don't insist if the host declines. Complimenting homemade food is always appreciated.

## Dress Code

Calabrians take pride in their appearance, so even casual outings are an occasion to dress smartly. When visiting churches or attending religious events, it's important to dress modestly. Women should cover their shoulders and knees as a sign of respect. At the beach, swimwear is fine, but it's not appropriate to wear it in town or at restaurants. Always bring a cover-up when leaving the beach.

## Religion and Cultural Respect

Religion, especially Roman Catholicism, plays a big role in Calabrian life. There are many religious festivals and events throughout the year. Attending one is a great way to experience the culture, but be respectful. When entering a church, dress modestly, speak quietly, and avoid taking photos during services.

Many businesses close during religious holidays, and Sundays are important family days when many small shops may be closed.

**Tipping and Money**
Tipping is not as common in Calabria as it is in other places. In restaurants, a service charge is often included in the bill, but leaving a small tip (5-10%) for good service is appreciated. At cafes or bars, rounding up the bill or leaving some change is polite.

# Sustainable and Responsible Travel in Calabria

Recently, Calabria has adopted sustainable travel practices to protect its environment, support local communities, and encourage eco-friendly tourism. As more people recognize the importance of protecting nature and respecting cultures, travelers to Calabria can enjoy this wonderful region while making a positive difference.

**Eco-Friendly Accommodations and Practices**
Sustainable travel in Calabria includes staying in places that prioritize eco-friendly practices. Agriturismos, or farm stays, allow travelers to experience local culture while reducing their

environmental impact. Many of these farms use organic methods, renewable energy, and water recycling to lessen their ecological footprint. Guests can also enjoy fresh local food and participate in traditional farming activities.

For those preferring a hotel, many accommodations in Calabria are adopting sustainable practices like reducing plastic waste, using energy-efficient appliances, and conserving water. Some hotels even have eco-certifications, ensuring they meet international sustainability standards. Travelers can choose accommodations that are committed to these practices to help lower their environmental impact.

**Supporting Local Communities**
Responsible travel also means supporting the local economy. Calabria's farmers, artisans, and small businesses are key to the region's culture. When visiting, consider shopping at local markets for handmade goods like ceramics and jewelry. Dining at locally-owned restaurants and buying food from regional producers also helps sustain the local economy and preserve

traditional Calabrian cooking and farming practices.

**Reducing Environmental Impact**
Calabria's natural beauty is fragile, and visitors can help protect it by being mindful of their impact. When exploring places like Sila National Park, Aspromonte National Park, or Tropea's beaches, follow the "leave no trace" principle—take your waste with you, stick to marked paths, and avoid disturbing wildlife.

Hiking, cycling, and swimming are great ways to experience Calabria's nature without causing harm. Guided eco-tours can teach visitors about the region's ecosystems and conservation efforts. To further reduce your environmental footprint, use trains or public transportation to travel around Calabria.

**Promoting Cultural Preservation**
Sustainable travel also involves respecting Calabria's cultural heritage. Travelers should be mindful of local customs, attend cultural festivals, and learn about the region's history. Participating in events like the Tarantella Dance Festival and visiting historical sites with care

can help preserve Calabria's unique culture for future generations.

## Important Contacts and Emergency Numbers

This section provides important contact information for emergencies, healthcare, transportation, and tourist assistance.

### 1. Emergency Numbers in Italy

Italy has a straightforward system for emergency services. Familiarize yourself with these numbers, which are accessible from any phone:

- *112* – General Emergency Number (European Union Emergency Number): Call this number for any emergency, including police, fire, and medical services. Operators often speak English.
- *113* – Police (Polizia di Stato): Use this number for non-emergency police help, like reporting theft or a missing person.

- *115* – Fire Department (Vigili del Fuoco): Call this number for fire emergencies or rescue services.
- *118* – Medical Emergency (Emergenza Sanitaria): Dial 118 for medical emergencies, including accidents and sudden illness. Medical staff in tourist areas often speak basic English.

## 2. Healthcare Services

Know these healthcare contacts, especially if you plan to stay long or engage in risky activities:

### Local Hospitals:
- Grande Ospedale Metropolitano Bianchi-Melacrino-Morelli in Reggio Calabria.
- Annunziata Hospital in Cosenza.
- Pugliese-Ciaccio Hospital in Catanzaro.

### Pharmacies (Farmacie):
Pharmacies are common and usually display a green cross. Many are open 24/7. Look for "Farmacia di Turno" for those open at night.

### Emergency Medical Assistance for Tourists:

Carry your insurance card if you have international coverage. Consider travel insurance that includes medical care. Your local consulate can also assist with healthcare needs.

### 3. Tourist Information and Assistance
For travel information or help, contact regional tourist offices:

*Tourist Office of Reggio Calabria:*
Located near the main promenade, and offers assistance in various languages.

*Tourist Information in Tropea:*
Helps with accommodations, excursions, and beach activities.

### 4. Transportation Services
For travel-related issues, use these contacts:

*Italian National Railways (Trenitalia):*
For train schedules, tickets, or lost luggage, call +39 06 3000 or visit their website. For domestic travel, use 89 20 21.

*Calabrian Bus Services:*

Bus services are run by companies like Autolinee Federico and Lirosi Autolinee. Check their websites or local bus stations for updated schedules. The bus station in Lamezia Terme is a major hub.

## 5. Consulates and Embassies

For consular assistance, contact your country's consulate or embassy:

*U.S. Consulate General in Naples:*

For American citizens, call +39 081 583 8111 for emergencies.

*British Consulate in Rome:*

British nationals can call the embassy in Rome at +39 06 4220 0001 for emergency services.

# Chapter 8
# Bonus Section
## Essential Italian Phrases for Travelers

When you visit Calabria, learning some basic Italian phrases will make your trip much better. In larger cities, many people speak some English, but in Calabria, which is more rural and authentic, English isn't as common as it is in places like Rome or Florence. Knowing key Italian phrases can help with everyday things like ordering food, asking for directions, and checking into hotels. It also helps you connect with locals, who appreciate it when visitors try to speak their language. Here are some important phrases to know before your trip:

### Greetings and Polite Phrases

Polite conversation is important in Calabria, where hospitality is highly valued.

- Buongiorno – "Good morning" (used until late afternoon).

- Buonasera – "Good evening" (used after 5 PM).
- Ciao – "Hi" or "Bye" (informal, used with friends).
- Arrivederci – "Goodbye" (more formal).
- Grazie – "Thank you" (use it often).
- Prego – "You're welcome" (common after saying *grazie*).
- Per favore – "Please" (when asking for something).
- Mi scusi – "Excuse me" (to get someone's attention).

## Asking for Directions

You'll likely need to ask for directions while exploring.

- Dov'è…? – "Where is…?" (e.g., *Dov'è la stazione?* – "Where is the train station?").
- A destra – "To the right."
- A sinistra – "To the left."
- Dritto – "Straight ahead."
- Quanto è lontano? – "How far is it?"

**Eating Out**

Calabrian food is a highlight, and knowing how to order makes it even better.

- Vorrei... – "I would like..." (e.g., Vorrei un caffè – "I would like a coffee").
- Il conto, per favore – "The bill, please."
- Posso avere...? – "Can I have...?" (e.g., *Posso avere dell'acqua?* – "Can I have some water?").
- Acqua frizzante o naturale? – "Sparkling or still water?"
- Quanto costa? – "How much does it cost?"

**Shopping**

Key phrases for shopping.

- Posso vedere...? – "Can I see...?"
- Quanto costa questo? – "How much does this cost?"
- Accettate carte di credito? – "Do you accept credit cards?"
- Vorrei comprare questo – "I would like to buy this."

**Emergency Phrases**

Important to know, just in case.

- Aiuto! – "Help!"
- Ho bisogno di un medico – "I need a doctor."
- Dov'è l'ospedale? – "Where is the hospital?"
- Chiamate un'ambulanza! – "Call an ambulance!"
- Sono malato/a – "I am sick."

**Miscellaneous Phrases**

- Non capisco – "I don't understand."
- Parla inglese? – "Do you speak English?"
- Va bene – "It's okay" or "Alright."

# Itineraries

### A Week in Calabria

Here's a simple itinerary for a week itinerary in Calabria:

## Day 1: Arrival in Reggio Calabria

Welcome to Calabria! Your journey starts in Reggio Calabria. After arriving at the airport, check into your hotel near the city center. Enjoy a walk along Lungomare Falcomatà, known as "the most beautiful kilometer in Italy," with views of the Strait of Messina and Sicily. Visit the National Archaeological Museum to see the famous Riace Bronzes and ancient Greek statues. For dinner, try local specialties like 'nduja at a trattoria.

## Day 2: Tropea – The Jewel of Calabria

Drive along the Tyrrhenian coast to Tropea. Explore the old town, visit the Sanctuary of Santa Maria dell'Isola, and relax on Tropea Beach. For lunch, enjoy fresh seafood, especially swordfish. In the afternoon, rent a boat to explore Capo Vaticano or go snorkeling.

## Day 3: Pizzo and Castello Murat

Travel to Pizzo, known for its cliffs, beaches, and historic sites. Tour Castello Murat, where Joachim Murat was executed, and explore the town's piazza. Don't miss Tartufo di Pizzo, a local ice cream dessert. Visit the Chiesetta di

Piedigrotta, a cave church with unique sculptures, and relax on Pizzo's beach.

### Day 4: Aspromonte National Park

Head inland to Aspromonte National Park. Start in Gerace, exploring its medieval architecture and cathedral. Spend the afternoon hiking in the park, looking out for wildlife. Return to a nearby village for a rustic Calabrian dinner.

### Day 5: Scilla and the Myth of Charybdis

Visit Scilla, a village linked to Greek mythology. Explore Ruffo Castle and Chianalea, the oldest neighborhood. Enjoy swordfish at a seaside restaurant, and relax on Scilla Beach or take a boat tour.

### Day 6: Stilo and Byzantine Treasures

Travel to Stilo to see the Cattolica di Stilo, a well-preserved Byzantine church. Explore Sila National Park, known for its lakes and forests. Consider hiking or biking in the park. End the day with dinner at a countryside agriturismo.

### Day 7: Relax in Lamezia Terme

Spend your final day in Lamezia Terme. Visit the Terme di Caronte for a relaxing soak in natural hot springs. Afterward, visit a local vineyard for a wine-tasting session. Enjoy a traditional Calabrian meal as you reflect on your trip.

# Calabria in 3 Days

### Day 1: Explore Reggio Calabria
Start your adventure in Reggio Calabria, a lively city with a mix of history, culture, and seaside beauty. Enjoy a leisurely breakfast at a local café with a cappuccino and pastry.

Visit the Museo Archeologico Nazionale di Reggio Calabria to see the famous Riace Bronzes, and ancient Greek statues that reveal the region's rich history.

Afterward, take a walk along the Lungomare Falcomatà seafront promenade. Enjoy views of the Strait of Messina and Sicily, and treat yourself to some traditional Calabrian gelato at a nearby café.

In the afternoon, explore the Castello Aragonese, a medieval fortress with stunning city and sea views. Imagine the history behind its walls.

For dinner, choose a local restaurant to taste Calabrian specialties like 'nduja, swordfish, or Pecorino cheese, paired with a glass of local wine.

### Day 2: Discover Tropea

On the second day, head to Tropea, known as the "Jewel of the Tyrrhenian Sea." Start your visit with a morning at Spiaggia di Tropea, one of Calabria's most beautiful beaches. Relax on the white sand or swim in the clear waters.

Next, explore Tropea's Old Town, with its narrow streets, charming shops, and vibrant markets. Don't miss the Sanctuary of Santa Maria dell'Isola, a church with stunning sea views.

For lunch, enjoy fresh seafood or traditional Calabrian pizza at a local trattoria. Try Tropea's famous red onions in a local dish.

In the afternoon, visit the Capo Vaticano area for its rugged coastline and beautiful views.

Relax at Grotticelle Beach or enjoy water sports.

Return to Tropea for dinner and savor the lively atmosphere. Try a dish featuring Tropea's sweet onions, like pasta or focaccia.

### Day 3: Explore Inland Calabria

On your final day, travel to Sila National Park, a beautiful area of forests, hills, and lakes. Drive through the park and walk around Lago Arvo for a peaceful experience.

If you enjoy hiking, try the Sentiero della Fiumara trail for stunning views and a bit of a challenge.

Afterward, visit Camigliatello Silano for a traditional Calabrian lunch. Enjoy local dishes like wild boar stew or chestnut desserts.

In the afternoon, head to Cosenza to explore its history and culture. Visit the Museo dei Brettii e degli Enotri to learn about ancient civilizations, and wander through the historic center.

Before leaving, shop for Calabrian souvenirs like local wines or handmade crafts.

End your trip with a farewell dinner, reflecting on your Calabrian adventure and savoring the region's flavors one last time.

# Conclusion

As we finish our exploration of Calabria, it's clear that this southern Italian treasure offers a unique mix of history, natural beauty, and rich culture. With its rugged coastlines, stunning mountains, and lively cities, Calabria showcases Italy's diverse charm. This guide aims to help you discover the essence of this amazing region and navigate its many treasures.

From the lively streets of Reggio Calabria to the peaceful beaches of Tropea, every part of Calabria shares a story of its history, culture, and natural wonders. Whether you're intrigued by the tale of Scilla and Charybdis, the medieval streets of Gerace, or the stunning views of Sila National Park, you'll find that Calabria's attractions are both varied and deep. The region invites travelers to enjoy local traditions and taste the unique flavors of Calabrian cuisine, going beyond just its famous sights.

Calabria is not just a place to visit but an

experience. This guide highlights some of the most captivating features of the region, from the coastal beauty of Capo Vaticano to the peaceful retreats of the Sila Mountains. Each chapter offers a thorough view of what makes Calabria special, ensuring your journey through this part of Italy is both memorable and enriching.

For those planning a trip, this guide offers practical tips, detailed itineraries, and a deeper understanding of the local culture and history. It's designed to help you discover Calabria's hidden gems as well as its famous landmarks. As you travel through this beautiful region, from historical sites to pristine beaches, you'll find that Calabria has a way of surprising and delighting at every turn.

By embracing Calabria, you embrace a place that is authentic and unspoiled, rooted in tradition yet welcoming to curious travelers. Its landscapes, cuisine, and people are intertwined in a story that is both ancient and fresh. Whether you are an adventurous traveler or someone seeking relaxation, Calabria offers a unique experience that will linger in your memory long after you leave.

As you get ready for your journey through Calabria, remember that this guide is more than just tips and information. It's an invitation to explore a region that blends history with modern life and tradition with innovation. May your travels be filled with discoveries, and may the beauty of Calabria leave a lasting impression on you.

Safe travels, and may your adventure in Calabria be as unforgettable as the region itself.

# THANK YOU FOR READING

YOUR FEEDBACK MEANS A LOT TO ME AS AN AUTHOR. IF YOU FOUND THE BOOK HELPFUL OR IT MADE A POSITIVE IMPACT ON YOU, COULD YOU PLEASE TAKE A MOMENT TO SHARE YOUR THOUGHTS IN A REVIEW ON AMAZON. YOUR HONEST REVIEW NOT ONLY HELPS ME GROW AS A WRITER BUT ALSO HELPS OTHER READERS DECIDE IF THE BOOK IS RIGHT FOR THEM. THANK YOU FOR YOUR TIME AND CONSIDERATION. YOUR SUPPORT IS GREATLY APPRECIATED.

BEST REGARDS
DAVID S. WEXLER

Made in the USA
Middletown, DE
27 June 2025

77563158R00076